6/23   2.F.

GW00392106

Deacon

Thomas Baker

 TWENTY-THIRD PUBLICATIONS
185 WILLOW STREET • PO BOX 180 • MYSTIC, CT 06355
TEL: 1-800-321-0411 • FAX: 1-800-572-0788
E-MAIL: ttpubs@aol.com • www.twentythirdpublications.com

Twenty-Third Publications
A Division of Bayard
185 Willow Street
P.O. Box 180
Mystic, CT 06355
(860) 536-2611
(800) 321-0411
www.twentythirdpublications.com

ISBN:1-58595-193-5
Printed in the U.S.A.

Contents

Introduction   5

A Work in Progress   9

Deacons in Theory and Practice   13

The Go-Between   22

Deacon's Family   32

Is It Working Yet?   38

Resources for Further Reading   45

Introduction

About twelve years ago now, when I first started telling friends and relatives that I was beginning the formation process to become a deacon, I'm sad to say I encountered a distinct lack of enthusiasm.

That may be a result of the kind of people I hang around with, who tend to be, shall we say, a little cynical when it comes to any kind of officialdom, especially in the church. In some cases, it was just a lack of familiarity with what deacons are and what they do. But in other cases, the people in question had (I guess) seen deacons in action, and they hadn't been particularly impressed.

I remember vividly one conversation I had with one of my closest friends, who rolled his eyes when I told him.

"What do you want to do that for?" he asked.

"I'm not sure," I said weakly. "It just seems like something I want to try."

"What do you get to do, huh? Say 'The Mass is ended, go in peace' every Sunday?" he said sarcastically.

"I don't know, I guess so," I replied.

He remained unimpressed, shaking his head. But then, his face brightened and he looked up. "Can you say it *at any point* during the Mass?"

I've always been grateful for this conversation, since it gave me my first (and only) deacon joke. But his first question What do you want to do *that* for?—had me stumped for a good long while.

I suppose anyone who begins any sort of unusual or unexpected phase in his or her life gets asked that a lot. And I felt as if I ought to have an answer, maybe even an inspiring one that could impress people. But for a long time, I didn't.

I did, of course, have a story to tell. I'd seen a few deacons over the years in various parishes, mostly performing assistant-like functions at liturgies. But I'd never known one personally, or done very much thinking about the purpose or history of deacons. Starting in college, I'd spent many years working in parish ministry as an avocation, mostly on liturgy committees, where I loved the process of preparation, rehearsal, and actual execution of the liturgies of the church year. As I hit my mid-thirties, I wanted something more from my involvement with parish and church ministry, but I wasn't at all sure what it was.

Eventually, I ended up in a one-priest parish where a generous pastor was eager to have some deacons. As a former journalist, I was interested in writing and wondered what it would be like to write and preach a homily. As a liturgy committee member, I was interested in being one of the actors in the play, and wanted to move on from my years as a liturgical stage manager, desperately gesturing instructions from the wings. So when the pastor asked me to consider studying for the diaconate, the timing seemed right. I entered the formation program, little knowing what I was getting myself into.

But "someone asked me to" didn't seem like a good enough answer to that big question of "Why?" I still wanted to be able to explain what deacons were for, and why I had to be one.

Nevertheless, I plugged along. But about two years into my formation program, I hit bottom with regard to the whole process. The classes had taken their toll on time with my young family. I was discouraged with a particularly uninspired semester of coursework, and disgusted with some ugly parish politics that didn't make the church seem like a place I wanted a more intimate relationship with. Tired, and uninspired, and still without my One Great Reason, I almost dropped the whole thing. It was time to decide about going forward with ordination, and I wasn't ready.

But a wonderful spiritual director I had at the time (who was pretty down on deacons herself) did a marvelous job of forcing the issue. "So what do you want?" she'd ask. "Why do you feel you need to stay?"

One night I blurted it out. "I don't have a reason," I said. "There often seems no point to it at all. The point is still being worked out. That's why I like it." I surprised myself, not only with my commitment to the idea, but with the discovery that it was not only OK, but a plus, that the idea of being a deacon didn't (for me) mean one great inspiring goal. I liked the idea that becoming a deacon was a search for something I hadn't seen yet, something that didn't have a well-defined role I could feel I'd achieved. The process of working out something new and unproven was a challenge in itself.

That's what it has come down to for me: the diaconate is a quest that has just begun. We don't really know yet what deacons are, or can be, or what role they will come to play in the church of the future. In a hundred years, deacons may turn out to have been an idea from the church's distant past that didn't revive quite the way it was supposed to; or, we may turn out to be the face of ministry that most Catholics, from week to week, experience most often, and to be people who invent new and unheard of ways for the church to be present in the world. There's nothing that guarantees either outcome: deacons are still very much an experiment, and we'll see if our existence turns out to be justified.

A WORK IN PROGRESS

Strictly speaking, "deacon" is a role in the church that doesn't need to exist. It's long been part of Christian tradition to have people called deacons, of course (more to come on that), but the fact is, all of a deacon's liturgical and sacramental work can be done by priests, and all of his other leadership tasks and ministries can and should be done by laypeople. There doesn't seem to be any special diaconate "turf." Why, you could ask, do you need deacons at all?

The only reason is that there's something here with possibility, some things that this odd mixture of roles we call deacons may turn out to be particularly good at doing. What are those things? We have some clues from our history, but frankly, we're still learning—and luckily, as deacons we often have the freedom and even the obligation to learn, to experiment, to try to define new forms of ministry and new ways to serve people. Deacons are here to find new and interesting and challenging ways to work both in the church and in the world, to be both ministers and parents, to be both members of the church's hierarchy and secular experts in our chosen fields. It's unusual and uncharted territory.

The freedom to explore that territory, to me, is a hallmark of how deacons can and should see their role. Although we're definitely part of the church's structure of ministries, more than most, deacons can head in a number of directions. Every deacon can create a unique mix of ministry within the church and outside the church, or can bring the presence of a church minister to places and situations we haven't even begun to think about. If you like the idea of being on a parish staff and doing parish ministry, you'll find a place as a deacon—but you'll also find a place if you're called to minister to business people in their offices, or to prisoners in their cells, or to the neglected anywhere, far from any rectory or parish staff meeting.

By nature, deacons live in the gaps of church life, with contradictory identities. Deacons are ordained clergy, yes, but they are (usually) also people with a job in the secular world. We minister in parishes but aren't (unless we choose) tied there by any reason of employment. We are subject to the authority and leadership of our bishops, but in many respects have the freedom to imagine a setting and a direction for our ministry that is unique to each of us. Contradictory identities can lead to confusion, and even lack of direction, but they can also bring possibility.

Please recognize that my approach to defining what deacons are, and what I like about the diaconate, is my own. There are plenty of other deacons who would define it differently, and perhaps more soberly. Training for the diaconate and decisions about how deacons are assigned to their work vary greatly from diocese to diocese. But this rather exciting identity crisis, this inability to nail down exactly what it is that we're about or where we're headed, may in fact not be temporary, or unique to my odd way of looking at the world. In fact, it may be an integral part of diaconate tradition.

Here is my favorite example of what I mean. Whenever I wonder what we're supposed to be doing as deacons, or I hear a definition of our future that's too limiting or parochial, I take a great deal of comfort from Scripture describing what we traditionally regard as the appointment of the first deacons (although not referred to by that title at all) in the Acts of the Apostles.

> Now during those days, when the disciples were increasing in number, the Hellenists complained against the Hebrews because their widows were being neglected in the daily distribution of food. And the twelve called together the whole community of the disciples and said, "It is not right that we should neglect the word of God in order to wait on tables. Therefore, friends, select from among yourselves seven men of good standing, full of the Spirit and of wisdom, whom we may appoint to this task, while we, for our part, will devote ourselves to prayer and to serving the word." (Acts 6:1–4)

Seems clear, yes? To "serve at table," the distribution of the community's goods, is the job of the deacon, so that the real apostles can do the work only they can do.

But—just four verses later—Stephen (one of these seven table assistants) is next mentioned, not doing his work inside the community with the widows, but "full of grace and power, did great wonders and signs among the people....they could not withstand the wisdom and the Spirit with which he spoke" (6:8,10). Later, after Stephen's martyrdom and the beginning of persecutions in Jerusalem, Philip, another of the seven,

> went down to the city of Samaria and proclaimed the Messiah to them. The crowds with one accord listened eagerly to what was said by Philip, hearing and seeing the signs that he did.... (Acts 8:5–6)

So there you are. If we look to this passage for the definition of what deacons do, we immediately find that these prototypical deacons immediately saw other work besides table service that needed doing, and had the initiative, and apparently the freedom, to do it—even if the neat division of labor between deacons and apostles seems to have broken down rather quickly. Assigned to one task, they quickly migrated to another, immediately blurring their identity and their role.

Two thousand years later, the diaconate is once again a bit of a mess—and filled with just as much opportunity for the Stephens and Philips of our day to make something new of it.

FOR YOUR REFLECTION

- What is your experience of deacons, at your parish or at other parishes?

- Up to this point, how would you describe deacons to someone who hadn't seen one before? Would it be as assistant priests, or assistants to priests? Would it be in terms of their role at the liturgy?

- Of the deacons who have impressed you favorably, what struck you about them?

- Does your local diocese have an active program to recruit and train deacons? Has it ever been made evident at your parish?

- As the number of priests declines, what gaps in parish ministry does that create? Who can best fill these roles? Does it need to be ordained people?

FOR YOUR PRAYER

Lord, you have inspired people in every place, and from every walk of life, to serve you and your people. You call us all to be leaders as well as followers, and to bring your gospel to every setting. Give your church the wisdom and imagination to create new ministries and roles, and to fill them with faithful and courageous people.

DEACONS IN THEORY AND PRACTICE

The definition you'll hear most often of what deacons do always sounds very neat: deacons *serve*. Most of the church's official documents define diaconal ministry as a ministry of charity, with a particular call to organize, spearhead, and energize the church's work in this area. Some writers even believe that the deacon's distinctive stole, worn over one shoulder, leaves one arm symbolically free to offer assistance—a sign of the ministry deacons are there to build.

What deacons currently do in reality, however, is a slightly different story. As we'll see, some deacons are in fact remarkable leaders in charitable undertakings, and a strong service-focused spirituality directs them to seek out this kind of ministry as their place. But in many other cases, deacons focus their ministries on, well, many of the same things other parish ministers do: planning and taking a role in the liturgy, preparing children and adults for the sacraments, teaching classes, sometimes administering programs or budgets or office work in the parish. In fact, a growing minority of deacons is serving as full-time parish administrators in the absence of a pastor. All these things are, of course, "service" to the church and its people—but perhaps not that original focus on works of charity and justice that is so often pointed to as the deacon's reason for being.

How did this rather confusing set of roles come to be? And what does it mean for our ability to give an answer to the question of what deacons actually "are"? That's what I hope to discuss in this chapter and the next as well.

In Theory: Diakonia

We do hear about people called "deacons" in the New Testament in one or two places, and even more about an idea called (in Greek) *diakonia*.

Let's return to that reading from the Acts of the Apostles just a few pages ago, the one that by long tradition tells us something about the differentiation of ministries in the early church that ultimately gave us people called deacons. When the Twelve said that their time could be better spent doing things other than "serving at table," the word they used for "serving" is the Greek verb *diakonein*. There we have it, some say: that is where we get the title and the office of "deacon," from this idea of direct, charitable service—quite literally, distributing food and support.

I've heard talks over the years about how the spirituality of the deacon and the identity of our ministry are firmly founded on this word and this very Scripture passage. As deacons, we serve.

> The outlines of the specific spirituality of the deacon flow clearly from his theological identity; this spirituality is one of service....In fact, with sacred ordination, he is constituted a living icon of Christ the servant within the Church. The Leitmotif of his spiritual life will therefore be service; his sanctification will consist in making himself a generous and faithful servant of God and men [sic], especially the

poorest and most suffering; his ascetic commitment will be directed towards acquiring those virtues necessary for the exercise of his ministry. (*Basic Norms for the Formation of Permanent Deacons*, 1998; para. 11)

In fact, deacons *do* serve. Many deacons I know are people of remarkable patience and energy in the traditional acts of charity they perform, from visiting the sick to ministering in prisons to running food-distribution centers to comforting the bereaved. If that word *diakonia* means, in part, the sleeves-rolled-up work of trying to be of direct assistance to people, many deacons, in fact, do *diakonia*.

But to what extent is service, and even leadership in service, meant to be the territory of deacons? Here we have to confront the issue of whether *all* the baptized aren't called to this same commitment to service and charity that we point to as the mission of the deacon.

The word *diakonia* in the New Testament, after all, doesn't just refer to that waiter-like "table service" in the Acts reading, that specialized work they had in mind for those first seven deacons. For example, in Mark's gospel, when we hear that "the Son of Man came not to be served, but to serve," it's the same basic Greek verb that's used. Jesus, along with all the apostles and all the leaders in the early church, engaged in *diakonia*, which in many other passages clearly refers to service much more broadly defined than table service and charity, perhaps as ministry, proclamation, preaching, and healing. It's hard, in fact, to define *diakonia* as anything other than the service of God and neighbor that is the daily business of every Christian—certainly not just deacons.

That's why it is rather dangerous to set up one ordained role in the church as *diakonia* specialists. If the evolution of our church since the Second Vatican Council has brought us anything, it is the knowledge that every one of the church's baptized members, whether or not they are ordained, shares the glory and the obligations of life as a follower of Christ. None of us can assign any of our basic duties to any other class in the church. Prayer, service, justice—we can't and won't delegate those to anyone else.

That could be one reason why the emergence of deacons as clear specialists in organizing and leading charitable endeavors hasn't really happened. At the same time as the diaconate was revived, *everyone* in the church felt more empowered to take leadership roles, particularly in acts of direct service. In my current parish, for example, the charitable work of the community is led, not by deacons and not by the pastor, but by dozens of laypeople (primarily, as in most parishes, generous women). They do a better job than I could ever do collecting food, coordinating with other local churches and relief agencies, and doing the hard, thankless work of phone calling, driving, and organizing. I feel no need to have a deacon in there pulling things together; most parishes I know aren't waiting around for a deacon to lead the charge here, either.

But in fact, although deacons are often defined in terms of this *diakonia* tradition, there were other, perhaps more significant reasons that the bishops and experts of the Second Vatican Council brought back the diaconate.

In Practice: Twenty-first Century Associates?

I hope everyone has read the wonderful novel *Morte d'Urban*, by the great American Catholic writer J. F. Powers, or at least some of his short stories. Still funny and perceptive despite being more than forty years old, these stories do a better job than any history text recalling what priestly and parish life was life in the years just before the Second Vatican Council.

No, you won't find any deacons in these stories. But what you will find is more to the point: priests, and lots of them, in every parish. In the stories of Powers, pastors have a constant supply of young assistant priests, who get pressed into service doing everything from taking the parish censuses to counting the collection. (There are so many priests, in fact, that some of them won't ever make it to be pastors, as in one of his most poignant and insightful stories, "Prince of Darkness.")

In most places in our country, nothing could be further from the current reality. My own parish has 1,700 families, and has (and will never have more than) one priest. With four Masses each

Sunday, about 200 baptisms a year, weddings, wakes, funerals, 150 children having First Communion annually—you get the picture. The math simply doesn't work. Pastors these days—and most of them know it—need help sharing the ministerial load of preaching, baptizing, marrying, and burying the dead. If deacons do nothing else right now, they are helping to fill the gap left by a generation of associate priests that simply isn't there.

I've heard many people in parishes come right out and say this: it's great that they have deacons now, because what is the church going to do without all those priests? People in the pews who see more and more deacons assume that this is the reason: deacons are simply needed to help make sure that the sacramental life of the parish continues. And while there are still pastors who for some reason resist the idea of welcoming deacons into their parishes, the vast majority is happy for the help. Without deacons, pastors in large one-priest parishes simply couldn't do all the baptisms, go to all the wakes, and chair all the meetings. Deacons help make a pastor's often-crazed life a bit more manageable.

Surely in many respects this is a noble calling, and it has the advantage of responding to a clear and pressing need. Those of us who want to pass on the gift of our church's sacramental life and symbols to our children know it won't happen by itself, and that at the key moments of our lives we want and need one of the church's ministers to be there with us. It is also, frankly, one of the reasons that the permanent diaconate was restored in our church. The current *Basic Norms for the Formation of Permanent Deacons* reminds us that

> [T]hree reasons lay behind this choice [to restore the diaconate]: (i) a desire to enrich the Church with the functions of the diaconate, which otherwise, in many regions, could only be exercised with great difficulty; (ii) the intention of strengthening with the grace of diaconal ordination those who already exercised many of the functions of the Diaconate; (iii) a concern to provide regions, where there was a shortage of clergy, with sacred ministers. ("Joint Declaration and Introduction," para. 2)

What I will say now, therefore, may get me into dangerous territory. I hesitate to voice what sounds like criticism of the huge contributions made in many parishes by deacons who are invaluable helps to their pastors. In some parishes, deacons retired from secular careers are the mainstays of parish administration; others are available to chair any organization that the pastor can't manage to get to, or oversee any program that's short of help. Deacons and their wives have made themselves indispensable in many parishes, and that's often all to the good.

But I wonder whether this use of the diaconate as a partial solution to the shortage of priests results in deacons doing work that can, and should, be done and led by the non-ordained. I've been at meetings with other deacons where one of them will proclaim the need for additional deacons in his parish because of all the work that needs to be done—but when asked what kind of work he's referring to, I'll hear nothing but projects that can just as well be done by laypeople. Running baptismal preparation programs and pre-Cana nights, teaching classes, organizing pro-life activities: these are not programs that need either a priest or a deacon to run them. Sometimes I even wonder if deacons, by being willing to serve in so many capacities at low or no pay, are actually holding up rather than pioneering evolution in the church, and making it less likely that the church will hire qualified, trained lay ministers to take paid parish positions at living wages.

Because deacons are ordained and do receive years of training, some of it quite excellent, deacons run two risks when they center their ministries on the parish. First, the very existence of deacons can easily reinforce a natural deference on the part of laypeople about taking a leadership role. Many parishioners will naturally assume that a deacon will do a better or more experienced job at whatever the task at hand might be—and a deacon may be easily be tempted to go along with this way of thinking, rather than do the hard work of identifying and training lay leaders. Secondly, sad to say, deacons' ordination and training can also result in a subtle clericalism just as objectionable as it has sometimes been in our church's history on the part of priests. I do occasionally hear deacons complain that laypeople "don't understand that we're ordained," and insist on being called "Deacon." They seek a separateness and deference that their ordination was not intended to impart.

This temptation to turn deacons into parish ministers, or into junior priests, is not only ultimately bad for laypeople and for the church, but it may prevent deacons from finding the distinct and unusual identity that is theirs alone. Cardinal Roger Mahony of Los Angeles pointed this out strongly in an inspiring address to deacons in 2000:

> I urge you to resist allowing the diaconal ministry to be co-opted....The deacon should be free to respond to immediate needs and demands of the poor, the disenfranchised, those without work, the sick at home or in hospital, the many who are neglected, forgotten, invisible in our neighborhoods and communities. The deacon should be well prepared to serve as an advocate for social justice concerns in the wider community and in the workplace, bringing a deeper awareness and a heightened consciousness to the community of faith which he serves. If the deacon becomes overly concerned with the affairs of the parish, we run the risk of losing what is the most crucial and distinctive element of his unique call to service—that for which he is ordained—just service....If the diaconal ministry becomes too closely linked to liturgical and parochial functions, what is diminished is the distinct and irreducible ministry of the deacon. ("Cardinal Mahony Addresses NCDC," *Deacon Digest*, September/October 2000)

Nothing Unique?

Despite those inspiring words, this chapter's effort to map out the territory of deacons, to answer the question of what deacons "do," might seem as if it has ended up with a no-man's-land rather than firm borders.

On the one hand, deacons clearly don't have (and shouldn't

have) a monopoly on *diakonia* in the church, called as we may be along with all the rest of God's people to engage in the work of charity. So we can't define the deacon's role solely in terms of engaging in that wonderful word *diakonia* that has given deacons themselves their name. On the other hand, deacons in reality often find themselves filling in for key sacramental and ministerial functions that in the past were undertaken by a larger number of priests. This is a worthy effort, but not something that helps us define what is unique about deacons, and not without pitfalls that can easily turn deacons into, simply, committed parish ministers.

But deacons' contrary identities, and lack of a clear "place," may be clues to where we really belong, which is in a state of tension: between church and world, between parish and work, between our place in the hierarchy and our place in the secular sphere. We spend our lives running between all these worlds, trying hard to bring the insights and wisdom and reality of each to the other. It's to that role of the deacon—perhaps our true "territory"—that I'd like to turn in the next chapter.

FOR YOUR REFLECTION

- Have you experienced deacons as "ministers of service"? Do the deacons you know seem to have a special commitment to *diakonia*?

- Who are the principal ministers of service in your parish? Who in the church inspires you with their commitment to works of charity?

- Is the church a better or a poorer place with fewer priests in each parish? Why do you think so?

- How well do you think the church has responded to the reality of fewer priests? What are the solutions that would be helpful in your own parish?

- If there were no deacons in your parish, where would their absence be felt first?

FOR YOUR PRAYER

Lord, your church is constantly changing and ever growing, and the need for ministers to preach your gospel and serve your people is always great. Help us to call forth from our communities people who have the courage and the endurance to be priests, the commitment to the church and to the world to live as deacons, and the generosity and patience to minister as laypeople.

THE GO-BETWEEN

If you're a deacon, you have to get used to a lot of little slights—mostly unintentional. Since deacons are still rare birds in some parishes and dioceses, many people aren't used to remembering that we exist, and we sometimes get left off lists, thank-you speeches, and invitations. It's just the way it is.

Recently, in a diocese near me, the existence of the diaconate was omitted from a published overview of the diocese that listed, in a table, the number of priests and professed religious (nuns and religious brothers), but not deacons. When a valiant deacon brought this to the attention of the fundraiser who had prepared the brochure, he was told, in explanation, "Well, after all, you guys are neither fish nor fowl."

You can imagine how well this definition of the diaconate went over. But it's an accurate portrayal of how many people see deacons: sort of clergy, sort of laypeople, really neither. Often, we're seen as compromise clergy, kind of a second-class citizen of the ordained world. One impressive, vibrant woman I met in an Episcopal parish who was considering pursuing the diaconate in her church told me that ultimately she wasn't sure why she'd choose to be a deacon when she could also be a priest: "It would be like being a nurse," she reasoned, "when you could just as easily be a doctor."

As I said, you have to put up with a variety of comments as a deacon. I'm sure you do when you're a nurse as well. But it does point out confusion (and not only in the Catholic church) about what's "special" about deacons, and why that fish-fowl impression is such a common one.

Rather than neither fish nor fowl, however, perhaps the secret to our identity and ministry is that we are both. Please don't picture the animal that would result—what I mean is that deacons do, in fact, lead double lives.

One Australian scholar, John N. Collins, has devoted an entire book (*Diakonia: Re-interpreting the Ancient Sources*) to tracing the origins and evolution of the word *diakonia*, not only back to the early church but to the Greek culture that preceded and helped to form our New Testament writers. He lays out the many ways in which the word "deacon" can mean servant, minister, even waiter. But he also points out settings in which the word means something more like "go-between": someone sent as a messenger from one home or town to another, an ambassador, someone whose job is to move back and forth.

This idea of deacons as "go-betweens" sounds right to me. What, after all, is the point of having members of the hierarchy who are also secular workers in the world, if they are not going to be official, dedicated ambassadors from each of those worlds into the other? Why have married clergy if we are not going to bring the insights of the married into the life of the church, and the beliefs of our church into the lives of families who may not be touched by other ministers?

This vision of deacons as messengers and intermediaries is not new. Deacons do not have a monopoly on acts of service and charity, but it may be their unique mission to bring news of the needs of the world to the church, and the message of the church to the secular world.

> The early metaphorical description of the deacon as "the eyes and ears, the mouth, heart, and soul of the bishop" referred to the duty of the deacon to identify the needy, to report their needs to the bishop and the Church, and to direct the Church's loving service of them...In our own day, Pope Paul VI has spoken of the deacon as being "the interpreter of the needs and desires of Christian communities...." (*Permanent Deacons in the United States: Guidelines on Their Formation and Ministry*, 1984; para. 35)

The schizophrenia of being a deacon—simultaneously living in the secular world and in the church's hierarchy—may be our real calling, interpreting the two worlds to one another. The rest of this chapter tries to describe the visible ministry of deacons inside the church, but also some ways that the deacon's "go-between" role is beginning to find expression.

Deacons in the Church

When I get asked what deacons "do," often what people mean is this: what is it that deacons "do" in the church, liturgically and sacramentally? Deacons, as ordained ministers, have specific roles in Sunday and other liturgies, and they are able to preside over the celebration of some (but not all) of the church's sacraments. This is the most visible "church" work that deacons do, and it is the way that, inside the church at least, people get to know who they are, what they believe, and what they are like.

Most deacons I know love and enjoy their ministry in the liturgy. Obviously there's a danger that deacons will see this as their primary role, and come to like being "up there" at the altar in a position of leadership more than they like the actual work of a deacon that makes their liturgical role meaningful. But through their work in the liturgy, deacons become visible and available people, and a deacon who doesn't enjoy his liturgical ministry will miss many opportunities to touch people's lives.

Among the things that deacons "do" are:

Proclaim the gospel. Deacons are the default readers of the gospel in any Sunday or daily liturgy. If there is a deacon present and vested, a deacon should read the gospel, taking precedence over any priest or even bishop who may be present.

Preach. Deacons are also permitted by canon law to preach, although in some cases a bishop can withhold this faculty if a particular deacon lacks the training or talent to speak effectively. How often a deacon preaches is usually worked out in consultation with the pastor in the parish where he serves. My experience has been that deacons are used as preachers enthusiastically by their pastors, who welcome the chance to preach less often and are thus able to spend more time preparing when they do preach.

Baptisms. Deacons are active as ministers of baptism in most parishes where they serve. In my parish, for example, the two deacons do all the baptisms, taking turns presiding at biweekly baptism liturgies with from one to seven or eight infants. As experienced fathers and child-handlers, most deacons are good at this work. Often, they'll instinctively know how to baptize a squalling child by immersion without drowning it, and can patiently tolerate the occasionally unruly baby (or family).

Weddings. Deacons are authorized to preside at wedding liturgies and bless marriages just as priests do. In these cases, deacons (often joined in this ministry by their wives) generally also take responsibility for meeting with the couple beforehand and guiding them through the marriage preparation process. In practice, deacons often focus on weddings involving a Catholic and a non-Catholic, since at a wedding of two Catholics there's usually a desire for a wedding Eucharist, rather than a wedding liturgy without Eucharist, at which a deacon can preside. However, even at a wedding Mass, a deacon may preside over the part of the liturgy when the couple exchanges their vows and rings.

Ministry of the Eucharist, especially of the cup. If you are an "extraordinary" minister of the Eucharist in your parish, maybe you'll enjoy knowing that deacons are "ordinary" ministers: that is to say, if they are present and available at a liturgy, they should always serve as ministers of the Eucharist even if there are enough lay ministers to take a deacon's place. Deacons, by long tradition, are particularly focused on the ministry of the cup, and should usually act as distributors of the consecrated wine in parishes where that option is offered. In parishes where communion is not offered in the forms of both bread and wine, it would be appropriate for deacons to take a leadership role in bringing this gift to the community.

Other Sunday duties. In a typical Sunday liturgy, if a deacon is present he will generally invite the congregation's responses during the penitential rite, announce the sign of peace, and pronounce the dismissal at the end of the liturgy. It's interesting to note that in these parts of the liturgy, the deacon's function is, in many ways, as a liturgical "go-between" between the presider and the people, making sure that the assembly's prayers and actions are announced and led.

Sing the Exsultet. During the course of the liturgical year, there are other ritual moments that require a deacon, particularly at the Easter Vigil. Each year, the great Easter proclamation called the Exsultet is sung at the beginning of the Vigil liturgy, just after the paschal candle has been solemnly carried into the church.

While anyone can sing the Exsultet in the absence of a deacon, this really is the deacon's big moment of the liturgical year, and while I often worry about whether or not

I'm up to the task, the honor of singing this ancient chant into a darkened church, lit only by the assembly's candles, is thrilling. Many deacons think they can't sing, and haven't worked on it much. Perhaps they haven't read liturgist Aidan Kavanagh's thoughts that "a deacon who cannot sing is like a reader who cannot read, a presbyter (which means elder) without age or wisdom, a bishop (which means overseer) who cannot see, a president who cannot preside" (*Elements of Rite: A Handbook of Liturgical Style*). Tough words that haven't found their way into many diaconate formation programs!

Beyond these liturgical duties, deacons' participation in the visible life of the church depends on their preferences, and the needs of the community they serve. Many deacons organize visits and communion calls to the sick or homebound; others regularly lead wake services at funeral homes, or play a role in other bereavement ministries. In many parishes, deacons lead regular morning and evening prayer services, sometimes in place of a daily Mass but more often as an additional liturgical option. In all these cases, deacons are not the only people in the parish who can take these leadership roles, but they are definitely places where a deacon can serve as a leader and organizer—and where the knowledge he gains of the community and its needs will make him a better preacher and parish minister.

Deacons Outside the Church

To fulfill their mission as go-betweens, though, deacons need to focus on problems and understand issues well outside of the church setting. Assisting at liturgy and ministering in the parish is wonderful, but in most parishes there is so much to do, and so many opportunities for a deacon to "sign up" for more and more liturgies, baptisms, weddings, and meetings, that the reason for the deacon's presence on the altar can be lost. Deacons have a liturgical role, after all, because they are to be a sign of how important their ministry of service, their role as "go-betweens," is to their community and to the church. They are on the altar because they are our representative ministers of charity and service, our messengers—not because we need their liturgical contributions to make the liturgy work.

So, if a deacon is to be the "eyes and ears" of both the bishop and the church, then it is his additional job to make sure that the realities and needs of the secular world of work and daily life find expression in the life of the church, and that the church can adequately reach out to people and places far outside the view of any parish.

To some extent, this go-between role happens by the very nature of the deacon's life. Many people don't realize that most deacons are entirely dependent on secular employment to support themselves and their families. Most don't receive any money or fringe benefits as a result of their ministry. (The few who do are usually retired from secular careers and working part-time in administrative roles on parish staffs.) So as a result, most deacons work outside the church full-time—and spend many more hours per week engaged in their secular occupations than they do in the "church" part of their diaconal ministry.

You might imagine that these two spheres of life, parish ministry and the typical religion-free American workplace, could easily remain separate. That, after all, is mostly how our society operates, with religion off limits as a topic of discussion or common ground during the week. But every deacon will tell you that the fact of their being a deacon has changed the way they are perceived in their place of work, and has opened up possibilities for ministering to people that would never have been there otherwise.

Primarily, this happens unexpectedly and unpredictably, and without overt proselytizing on the part of the deacon. Over time, people in a workplace come to hear that Fred is a deacon, and they mentally file that information away. One day, at lunch with Fred, the topic of capital punishment will come up, and Fred's opinion may be sought out simply because people wonder how the opinion of a "minister" fits in with the general consensus. Or, one of Fred's casual friends in the workplace will suddenly decide that because Fred seems to take religion seriously, it's OK to steer an informal conversation toward mentioning the pain of a failed marriage, or to ask where to turn for help.

These are moments of grace that don't need a deacon to minister to the other person—but they happen simply because of that added element of "official" identification as an ordained minister. Frankly, being a deacon is strange and unusual enough that it makes people wonder what goes on in your life, and that added element of curiosity can open doors. They don't need to be forced open, and most deacons don't use the workplace as a place to take inappropriate initiatives to start religious discussions.

But in addition to helping people one-on-one in the workplace, there are many creative ways—most yet to be invented—where deacons can and do fulfill their mission as go-betweens, as indispensable intersections between the secular and religious worlds.

Some deacons, for example, have built their ministry around much more formalized programs designed to reach people in their workplaces. In the Diocese of Paterson, New Jersey, deacons have helped to create a program in Work/Life Ministry at Seton Hall University, where they and others study the moral and justice issues faced in the workplace and create ways to minister to working people effectively. They organize meetings where business people at every level can meet and reflect on the significance of the career choices and business decisions they make.

Deacons have a special responsibility to break down the barriers that separate what we say and think on Sunday from what we do the rest of the week. The fact is, basic questions of honesty and justice confront people in the workplace every day: should I fake the sales results or the progress report the way I was asked to? Do I offer medical benefits to part-time workers, even if it means lower profits? Should I make a greater effort to hire disadvantaged people in my store? These are truly the front lines of the battle for justice, and we often forget that the place where many of our country's poor and disenfranchised are going to find real help is not in soup kitchens, necessary as they are, but in the businesses and workplaces operated by the people of our churches and communities.

Deacons often have the advantage of knowing the business world firsthand, and at the same time they've made a public and permanent commitment to the church's search for justice. They are in a wonderful position to run interference between these two places—helping open the eyes of working people to the significance of what they're doing, and helping the church to see where the real needs for teaching and evangelization lie.

Many deacons also find ways to use their specific secular career expertise in the cause of justice and charity. Advertising executives help raise awareness of social needs; carpenters and contractors organize building projects and train workers who otherwise couldn't get a start on a career. Not that every deacon needs to have the kind of career skills that lend themselves to this kind of immediate application to a ministry—but finding unusual ways to bring the secular world to the church, and the church to the world, is definitely our task.

These are not the only models for what deacons can or should be doing. But they do offer some hints and suggestions of how the job of the deacon is to be both very much in the church but also outside of it, not a priest with less authority but something entirely different, a person with a commitment to both church and world, both liturgy and work.

In short, if you're looking for a particular role in parish ministry, you can find one in any number of ways, such as volunteering or getting a degree in ministry. But if you like the idea of living at the intersection of where the church meets the world, and finding your unique way of making them one, then being a deacon is one place to live out that vision.

- How effectively do you think the church ministers to working people? to business executives? to government leaders?

- Have you experienced deacons preaching in your parish or in other parishes? Do you find that their preaching seems any different given their family life, or their status as full-time people in the working world?

- What do deacons do in your parish? Which of their jobs could be done by laypeople?

- What kinds of ministries or programs could help people reflect on the choices of career they make? the decisions they make at work about hiring or firing or promoting? the honesty with which they deal with people?

- Have you ever "held back" from having a conversation with someone at work if it was moving in the direction of faith or religion? Are people where you work aware of your commitment to your faith? If not, why? Would you be comfortable if they were?

FOR YOUR PRAYER

Lord, you created your church not as a place apart, but as your people, active in many places, many jobs, and many ways of life. Give your ministers the grace and the openness to put aside their desire for rank and honor, to bring the gospel to people in homes and schools, in offices and factories, in boardrooms and meeting rooms. Help us all to find new ways to participate with you in building the kingdom wherever you lead us.

THE DEACON'S
FAMILY

I 've hardly mentioned one of the most distinctive features of
the ministry and status of deacons in the Catholic church:
most of us are married.

That, of course, makes us a bit unusual among the church's
ordained ministers. In fact, sometimes it leads to misunderstand-
ings. On the one extreme, the occasional parishioner unfamiliar
with deacons is clearly shocked sometimes after Mass, when one
of my daughters rushes up to me in my vestments and starts calling me "daddy." (The look of speechlessness on the person's face
is, in some cases, priceless.) At the other extreme, some people
assume that the diaconate is the way the church is going about the
business of a married priesthood: we're just calling them deacons,
and giving them less authority than regular priests.

As we saw in the last chapter, deacons aren't priests—we have a different mission in life and in the parish. But we do have families, and no matter how we exercise our ministry our wives and families are, for better or for worse, affected by the commitments we make and the lives we lead. No deacon, in fact, can be admitted to ordination without the firm and enthusiastic commitment of his wife—who by that time, after years of formation, will probably have a pretty good idea of what she's getting involved with.

Being a deacon's family isn't an exact parallel with the experience of being a minister's family in a Protestant church. As deacons we and our families are not nearly as visible or subject to as much scrutiny as any pastor's family is, and since deacons earn their keep in the secular world we're not seen as employees or "staff" that can be hired or fired. But many of the same pressures that Protestant clergy's families experience do emerge—as well as some of the same inestimable benefits. Let's look at each in turn.

The Time Crisis

First and foremost, the commitment that a deacon's wife and family makes to this ministry is time—not their time, necessarily, but time when their deacon/father/husband is away from home.

Being a deacon can become a time-management nightmare, for both him and those around him. In fact, the problems often emerge early, even during the formation program, which can be a more intense and inflexible commitment than ministry after ordination. Most programs now require more than 1,000 hours of instruction and experience over the course of four to five years, generally involving in-person attendance at a local college or diocesan center. The commitment can involve several long nights a week for multiple years, as well as occasional weekends for special classes, retreats, or other activities. With a full-time job, the sudden addition of this new commitment can create some immediate stresses, as wives fill in the gaps caused by their husbands' absences and distractions—and no matter how you prepare yourself for it intellectually, the reality of any new commitment often turns out to be more powerful than you imagine.

Some deacons, of course, have no children or grown children, and for them the time commitment can include their wives rather than create a burden for them. Many formation programs not only permit but encourage wives to attend virtually every class or workshop along with their husbands. For many older couples going through the formation process, it's clearly something they enjoy doing together—perhaps, in fact, the most time they've been able to spend together on a common endeavor in their entire married lives.

That's one role model for being the deacon's wife: a visible and constant companion, not only in the formation process but in the parish as well. Some spouses of deacons are as active and well known in their parishes as their husbands, and partner with them in many ministries, such as marriage and baptism preparation. This obviously helps alleviate some of the potential conflicts around the management of a deacon's time (although it may also create other problems as the couple becomes a highly visible "model marriage" and may in fact try to impose this model on others around them).

But it's important for all deacons and their wives to know that this isn't the only model of integrating the diaconate into their marriage. Some wives of deacons, although completely supportive of their husbands' vocation and commitment, choose not to share their training or ministry in any direct way. They work hard and make major sacrifices to fill in and manage during their husbands' time devoted to ministry, but rather than become part of a "deacon couple" they prefer to concentrate on their own careers, raising children, or both. Frankly, my wife and I were put off by the intense vision of joint involvement that many deacons told us about when we started the formation process, since with two (later three) small children, we had problems enough on our hands. We were relieved to find that just as there are (or can be) many ways to be a deacon, their wives too can define their roles differently as they see fit.

In fact, some wives find that even a more limited role causes problems they hadn't expected. For example, some, like many other Catholic women, find it difficult to give equally enthusiastic support to every part of the church's teachings and discipline, especially as they affect women. What does that mean if you're married to a deacon and get asked your opinion? Will there be opinions or feelings you can't share in a prayer group or meeting because you're the deacon's wife? If the pastor has offended you, will you nevertheless be able to swallow hard and be civil to him when that's called for? These are real situations where a deacon's family has to weigh its own self-respect and honesty against the need to be supportive.

Is there a solution to every pressure and problem that puts stress on a deacon's marriage or family? Obviously not—and some of the stresses they face will be entirely apart from (and perhaps predate) any issue related to the diaconate. But most deacons come to realize that their commitment to their families is far more important than any specific commitment they've made in their ministry, and that the power of saying "no" is the first gift the Holy Spirit should give to us at ordination. As a deacon, you don't need to make the same time or liturgical commitments as any other deacon in your parish, even though at times you'll want to or feel pressure to or maybe even be told to. And when the ministry or project you love begins to take its toll on you or your family, hopefully you'll have the wisdom to back off—and the gift of a wise spouse to tell you to.

Where Would We Be without Them?

That brings us, in fact, to the many pluses of being a deacon with a family. This could easily be the longest section of this little booklet, filled as it would be of praise for my own wonderful wife, three sharp-eyed, funny, brilliant daughters, and the many other great friends I've met in the families of my fellow deacons. But rather than subject you to that, here is just one reason why the ministry of deacons benefits so much from their having a family alongside them: the gift of honesty and insight from people close to you.

I'm sure there are many benefits that accrue to those who have chosen the celibate life. But frankly, I don't know how priests survive without a wife to look at their homilies beforehand, and some children to tell them what it all sounded like afterwards. Because your own immediate family knows you so well, and has seen you at your best and at your worst, they're equipped with some amazing and infallible antennae. They know what you're really like. They can, if you let them, alert you when you've gone off the deep end in one way or another.

Your family may well be the first to see when you're taking your role as a deacon a bit too seriously, or are lecturing from on high rather than preaching from the gospel, or are spending too much time hanging around the rectory. They know when you sound condescending, and when you stop practicing what you preach. They quietly but constantly remind you that you have other roles and obligations besides being a deacon, and that what you accomplish (or fail to) as a minister isn't the be-all and end-all of your life. Frankly, that's liberating.

All this is no guarantee that deacons will always be right on when it comes to talking about the issues that they, theoretically, will be closer to than priests: money, marriage, children, work, the Monday-through-Friday grind. Deacons have all the failings that other people have, all the inability to see their own faults, all the blindness to an opportunity to do good that's staring them right in the face. But they do have one advantage: people who know them and see them, all day every day, and can call them on it.

Most deacons depend, and happily so, on the good judgment and honesty of their wives and children. I suppose it's possible for a family to be so blindly supportive that they'd never tell you the truth about your platitudinous homilies and your pretentious role-playing. But I haven't seen one yet.

FOR YOUR REFLECTION

- What do you think the pluses are of deacons being married? the minuses? How would you answer those two questions if they referred to priests rather than deacons?

- What are your experiences with married clergy, and their families, in other Christian traditions or other faiths?

- Do you think deacons can be effective ministers given their many other time commitments? How do you think these time pressures affect the way they might approach their relationship to the church?

- Do you think deacons get training as thorough and as intense as priests do? Should they?

FOR YOUR PRAYER

Lord, you bring people together in marriage to support and love one another, to make promises of commitment and fidelity, and to share their love with children and the world around them. Bless all those who are married who are also serving the church in ministry, in the Catholic Church and in the many other Christian traditions with married clergy and ministers. Give them generosity with their time and talents, and a willingness to widen the circle of their families to include those who are forgotten and alone. Also give them judgment and wisdom to preserve and treasure their love for one another in the face of the needs and demands they face each day.

IS IT WORKING YET?

So, after about thirty years of having deacons back as a part of the life of our church, let's ask the practical, impatient American question: is it working?

In many ways, of course, the answer is: yes. Clearly, deacons are filling a need. In the diocese where I work, there are record numbers of candidates coming forward for formation, and more pastors see an immediate need that they trust deacons to fill. So inevitably, deacons are going to be a more visible part of church life, and it's not hard to foresee a day when the number of deacons, in some places, exceeds the number of priests and pastors.

But numbers only tell part of the story. There is still a long way to go before deacons reach their full ministerial potential. There are countless ways to be a deacon—not an assistant pastor, not a parish helper, but a deacon—that haven't been explored as yet.

With only thirty years of a revived diaconate behind us, you have to assume that the diaconate is a story that hasn't even finished its first, preliminary chapter.

What will the future as a deacon be like? Obviously I don't know, and it's not for me to decide. But here are a few closing reflections on ways that the diaconate may evolve in the future—if people come forward as deacons who want to take us in these directions.

Out of the Parish

As we've seen, due to the need for more and more ministers in our parishes, deacons have become indispensable pastoral associates. But deacons, as ministers of service and interaction with the world, may not all belong on parish staffs, organizing parish activities. This focus on the parish may ultimately hold back the invention of new forms and places of diaconal ministry where we would truly begin to see the distinction between deacons and priests, as deacons find settings for ministry that are totally outside the places where priests have traditionally served.

The way that many diaconate programs are currently structured reinforces the focus of deacons on parish ministry. To be accepted in a formation program, for example, you must be sponsored by a pastor, and after ordination subject to his continuing oversight. It's only natural that this would create an expectation that you'll serve under his direction and assist him in his tasks. Some pastors even refer to the deacons assigned to their parishes as "my" deacons—an unfortunate result of the way deacons are chosen and assigned.

As we get more and more deacons, perhaps the immediate need to put them all to work in parishes will be sated, and some other less parish-centered forms of diaconal ministry will emerge. Bishops may begin to work directly with deacons, and ask them to form organizations dedicated to workplace ministry, or issues of economic justice, or the analysis or awareness of social problems. In this way, deacons might return to one of their original roles, that of the "the eyes and ears, the mouth, heart, and soul of the bishop" (*Permanent Deacons in the United States: Guidelines on Their Formation and Ministry*, 1984; para. 35).

Women Deacons?

As everyone knows, Rome has declared the discussion of admitting women to the priesthood over and done with. But the ordination of women as deacons is, while not likely in the near future, an entirely separate question and one which is not closed.

The debates about whether there were women deacons in the early church are controversial, and perhaps ultimately beside the point. (Although it seems hard to overlook Paul's reference to "Phoebe, a deacon of the church at Cenchreae" in Romans 16:1–2, as well as other passages.) The real issue is whether the reasons that the church denies the priesthood to women also apply to the diaconate. There has been little discussion of this in recent years, although the many Vatican documents related to women and the priesthood in the 1990s carefully omitted any mention of the diaconate.

Much of the resistance to women deacons is based on a fear that it would create an expectation that women priests wouldn't be far behind. Certainly there are pastors, and perhaps some parishes, who would find it hard to accept an ordained female deacon. But at some point, perhaps a vision of the opportunity, rather than the risks, will carry the day. For my part, I can't imagine a change in discipline that would bring more life to the church, and more promise for its future. Certainly, if one of the goals of the restoration of the diaconate was to "strengthen...with the grace of diaconal ordination those who already exercised many of the functions of the Diaconate" (*Basic Norms for the Formation of Permanent Deacons*), we can't deny that women today are just as likely to be exercising those functions as men.

I'm sure I don't speak for all deacons when I say a word in favor of women joining us, but it's hard not to discuss the diaconate without it. Maybe it's just that I'm tired of explaining all this to my daughters, but I think it's a change that would make me a happier deacon.

Deacons without Boundaries

I've had the good fortune over the past few years to meet and work with people serving as deacons in several other Christian denominations. In some traditions, the title "deacon" doesn't designate someone who has been ordained, but especially in the Episcopal church the life of the diaconate has much in common with the experience in the Roman church: recent restoration and increasing popularity, together with frequent confusion about what makes for a priest as opposed to what makes for a deacon.

I wonder if there will be some ways in which deacons can reach across denominational boundaries and discover that it makes sense to work together. We share not only our common experience in trying to rebuild and define the diaconate in our churches, but the same commitment to justice and charity, the same commitment to reaching outside of the usual places for church ministry. It's not hard to imagine deacons in a large city from every denomination deciding to commit themselves to a joint effort in ministry—or, at the very least, some regular meetings and discussions.

Still Working It Out

A few weeks before my ordination, along with my classmates, I went on a retreat that was to be among our last joint activities before the big event. We were all excited, glad that the years-long preparation process was finally going to be over, but also anxious about what was going to be expected of us. How much time would it really take? How would people respond to us? Most importantly, did we really have anything to contribute to this ministry that sometimes sounds so intimidating? How can anyone really be up to the standard of being the church's ordained ministers of service and charity?

I wound up in a casual, one-on-one discussion with one of the "veteran" deacons who were with us on the retreat. He was not someone I'd been particularly friendly with up to that point, and he'd never seemed very communicative. But we talked about what his life after ordination had been like, and what people's expectations of us as deacons were really going to be. He gave me some terrific advice that I've remembered to this day, and of course it applies to any ministry, not just being a deacon: "You can't worry about some model that means you're going to help everybody. You're not. Some people may be affected by your work and a lot won't be. The greatest gift you can give as a deacon is simply to be who you are. Your personality, the things you are interested in and passionate about—that's what will help people."

Being a deacon has its frustrations. It often isn't easy to have a role that so many people seem so confused about. But it is a ministry that has room for you to be who you are, and to define how you want to serve people in a way that reflects who you are at your best. That alone makes it a wonderful opportunity. So if you're thinking about becoming a deacon, remember that your vision of what it can be can become part of what it actually is. And if you're not going to be a deacon, just be nice to us: we're doing the best we can trying to work this out.

FOR YOUR REFLECTION

- What are some settings for ministry that you feel the Catholic church, or your parish specifically, neglects?

- Do you feel your parish's ministries are too parish-centered? Where, and to what groups, would you like to see the church reach out?

- Have you experienced deacons outside of the Catholic Church? What are your impressions?

- Would you be open to women deacons in your parish? Why or why not? How would your pastor react? The other deacons in your parish? Your fellow parishioners?

- What if women were admitted to the diaconate, and the priesthood continued to be reserved to men? Would that be a change the church should welcome?

- How would you respond to the question, "Was it a good idea to bring back permanent deacons?"

- If you are a deacon, is there a particular direction you would personally like to take your diaconal ministry?

FOR YOUR PRAYER

Lord, for hundreds of years your church has called forth deacons in your service, in ministries and settings that are ever-changing, but with a common commitment to serving your people in whatever place they are needed. Help us to remember that the future, not the past, is where deacons and all your people are called to serve. Give those who are called to the diaconate some share in the energy, the creativity, and the courage of Stephen, Philip, Phoebe, and the other saints who have served you.

Resources for Further Reading

There are only a few good books or periodicals dedicated to the diaconate. That will change over time as the number of deacons in our country grows beyond the current 12,000, and as deacons themselves, with experience, offer more reflection and perspective on what the diaconate can accomplish.

Among the few good books that do exist, James Monroe Barnett, in *The Diaconate: A Full and Equal Order* (Valley Forge, PA: Trinity Press International, rev. ed. 1995), writes from an Episcopal perspective and provides a thorough history of the diaconate from the early church onwards. John N. Collins' *Diakonia: Reinterpreting the Ancient Sources* (New York: Oxford University Press, 1990) focuses more on the word *diakonia* and its relationship to our understanding of ministry.

Aidan Kavanagh's *Elements of Rite: A Handbook of Liturgical Style* (Collegeville, MN: Pueblo, 1982) has a few valuable comments about deacons in the liturgy, and in general should be part of any basic liturgy bookshelf.

The United States Conference of Catholic Bishops' Secretariat for the Diaconate offers access to many of the official documents and guidelines related to the diaconate, and can point you to new books and resources as they become available. Basic documents as of this writing include *Basic Norms for the Formation of Permanent Deacons* (1998) and the American bishops' 1984 *Permanent Deacons in the United States: Guidelines on Their Formation and Ministry*. A new U.S. document on diaconal formation is expected soon.

The USCCB website is at http://www.nccbussb.org/deacon,

and their mailing address is 3211 4th Street, N.E., Washington, DC 20017-1194.

Deacon Digest magazine does not seem to be professionally edited, but at least offers listings of and reports from diaconate events and convocations, and sometimes has interesting news of how different deacons are living their ministry. Information is available at http://www.nccbuscc.org/deacon/digest.htm, or by mail at 502 George Street, DePere, WI 54115.

For a perspective on how countries other than the United States are experiencing the diaconate, the International Diaconate Centre, based in Germany, has a website at http://www.kirchen.de/drs/idz.

If you are exploring the diaconate as a possible direction for your own vocation, your best path is simply to establish contact with deacons in your area. Take a deacon to lunch, and ask about how he experienced the formation process, and how diaconal ministry is envisioned and led in your local diocese. Most, but not all, dioceses in our country have active diaconate formation programs, and your diocese's diaconate office can provide information, advice and guidance, and details on your local church's particular requirements and guidelines.